E
FOR

3 3434 00157364 3
Ford, Miela.

Sunflower

SUNFLOWER

by Miela Ford
pictures by Sally Noll

Greenwillow Books New York

Gouache paints were used for the full-color art. The text type is Futura Light.
Text copyright © 1995 by Miela Ford. Illustrations copyright © 1995 by Sally Noll.
All rights reserved. No part of this book may be reproduced or utilized in any form or by any means,
electronic or mechanical, including photocopying, recording, or by any information storage and
retrieval system, without permission in writing from the Publisher, Greenwillow Books, a division
of William Morrow & Company, Inc., 1350 Avenue of the Americas, New York, NY 10019.
Printed in Singapore by Kim Hup Lee Printing Co. Pte. Ltd.
First Edition 10 9 8 7 6 5 4 3 2 1

Library of Congress Cataloging-in-Publication Data
Ford, Miela.
Sunflower / by Miela Ford ; pictures by Sally Noll.
p.   cm.
Summary: A young girl plants a sunflower
seed, waters it, and watches it grow.
ISBN 0-688-13301-0 (trade).
ISBN 0-688-13302-9 (lib. bdg.)
[1. Sunflowers—Fiction.]   I. Noll, Sally, ill.   II. Title.
PZ7.F75322Su   1995   [E]—dc20
94-7547   CIP   AC

For my children,
Jeneva and Max
—M. F.

For Ava and Susan
—S. N.

I hold a seed
in my hand.

It is white with
dark stripes.

Carefully I place
it in the ground.

Every day I water it.

Every day I watch and wait.
Then, little green leaves.

Up to my knees.

Up to my nose.

Over my head.

Big yellow petals
face the sun.

Seeds in
the center.

Treats for
the butterflies.
Treats for the birds.

Treats for me.